JUMPSTART
REAL ESTATE
INVESTING

A 30 DAY ACTION PLAN TO
BUYING YOUR FIRST PROPERTY

NATASHA DONERSON BOWEN

FOREWORD BY
HULET T. GREGORY

ISBN: 1456327585
EAN13: 9781456327583

*This book is dedicated to
my beautiful daughter, Naomi
and my wonderful husband, William.*

CONTENTS

FOREWARD

Natasha came to me several years ago with a goal to start investing in real estate to grow wealth and eventually leave her "day job." Assisting Natasha in her real estate investing career has been very rewarding, but not as much as seeing her today–stepping up as a coach to "pass the baton" to others who also want to obtain financial rewards through real estate. Over the years I've learned that Natasha has what many people don't and what successful people do have: **a sense of urgency to get things done**!

Most people dream of financial freedom, but very few will ever take the steps to move forward. For many of those that do take that step forward, they fail. Why? Some reasons, I believe, are that they did not have a coach, nor did they surround themselves with people who were already successful in that field. For example, if you want to be a great doctor you need to go to medical school and be trained by doctors. That's a basic formula for success. However, when it comes to real estate most people will not follow that simple formula!

I personally know that Natasha has an impressive educational background with Bachelor of Science degree and a Masters in Business Administration. Even more, she was one of the top representatives in the country when she was in pharmaceutical sales. Make no mistake--Natasha's passion and drive to succeed is something that is not taught in any school or Fortune 500 company; it is her mind-set. If you really want to succeed and achieve your goals you have to change your mindset. Reading this book is the first step. I challenge you to read many more books about successful business people and real estate investing; you are what you read!

I got into real estate investing when I was 33 years old with one goal in mind: quit my job! After buying my first house for $17,000, 120 days later I had purchased 3 more single-family homes, and 2 large commercial office buildings. As a result I replaced a $130,000 salary as an executive of one of the nation's largest financial institutions. At the age of 35, I was a multi-millionaire and financially independent. I contribute to my success by surrounding myself with the right people and building a great TEAM. You will learn key details about this aspect from Natasha in this book. I continue to _operate_ very hard day-to-day with my various Real Estate companies and work with hundreds of investors all over the US and around the world. Did you catch that I used the word "operate" versus "work" in the above sentence? Making tons of money in real estate investing is not work to me. While it does take long hours and sacrifices to continue building my wealth, I look forward to the day of looking back at those I've helped and the opportunities to give back financially to various organizations. I know if you can only get a small part of what I have out of Real Estate Investing it will change your life forever!

At the timing of this book, real estate is the driver that has caused the worst recession since the Great Depression. To get into real estate now would be frowned upon by most, but the saying goes, *"Get Out when everyone is getting in and Get In when everyone is getting out."* Well everyone is getting out of real estate, so what should you be doing? My team and I have purchased over 1,000 properties in the last 6 years, and I can attest there is no time like the present to hit the ground running in real estate. Growing wealth in real estate is a long-term commitment; those who can take the basics from this book will be more likely to move forward with their goals and achieve success. I can assure you that I took these same steps in the beginning of my investing career. As you may have heard before, "talk is cheap," and indeed it is. However, this book will not only challenge you to change your mindset and thought patterns, but also to take action. Action is powerful and has value. Action is your work towards your destination. This book will empower you to take action one day at a time towards your destination of financial freedom! Remember, don't just talk-the-talk, walk-the-walk! The book you are about to read will not only give you the steps needed, but also hold you accountable for taking action!

I was honored by Natasha's request to introduce you to this book and want to congratulate you on making a decision towards reaching your financial and professional goals in Real Estate Investing!

Hulet T Gregory, President
Memphis CashFlow, GP
H&J Properties, LLC
Gregory Realty, LLC
Marathon Management, LLC
Marathon Realtors, LLC

CHAPTER 1

WHY 30 DAYS TO BECOME A REAL ESTATE INVESTOR

The only difference between a rich person and poor person is how they use their time.

Robert Kioyasaki

It has been proven that it takes 30 days to break a habit, but what does that have to with becoming a real estate investor? Just think about that for a moment. If you can make changes in order to lose weight, quit smoking, or to stop gambling all in the name of living a better life, taking 30 days to launch a new venture should be easy. Right? The answer is no, but I must admit that it is not that difficult. I have taken more than ten years of investing in real estate along with the lessons of other investors to make getting off to a great start very simple. I have found that when someone takes on a lot at one time it can be overwhelming. On the other hand, breaking down a huge task into small increments will insure completion by more than 80 percent. So everything you need to put in place to become a successful real estate investor is made simple with action steps for the next month. This book is your coaching manual to get you past your fears in order for you to take action. After the next 30 days, you will launch into a world to which you never thought you could gain entrance or never had the courage to try.

If you are reading this book you probably already believe in the possibilities of investing in real estate or are curious to find out what all of the late night infomercials are talking about. No matter the reason, you are ready to get started. It is true that when you compare the different investment vehicles, real estate has some major advantages. I will briefly cover the top five.

1. Passive Income

Rental property can provide you a steady stream of passive income. Monthly rent payments from tenants in excess of mortgage payment, taxes, insurance, and maintenance costs provide positive cash flow. Whether you or a management company manages the property, the collected payments are automatic cash flow to you that is considered income. Even more, over time as the mortgage remains constant, it is likely that inflation and housing demand will drive up rents that will increase your cash flow. It is important to emphasize, mind you, that there is no guarantee of profit in real estate investing. The value of real estate does not "always" rise—it merely tends to, and even then over the long haul, not necessarily either steadily or over the short term. At the time of writing—mid-year 2010—many parts of the United States have experience *lowered* residential real estate prices. This is a boon for today's buyer. But, equally, this fact is evidence that some residential real estate investors have failed to make money or increase the value of their holdings, and that some have lost. It is the naïve investor who believes that "real estate always goes up." It is the intelligent that acts with a combination of reasoned boldness and caution, with knowledge, research, and careful planning.

2. Appreciation

Appreciation is the increase in value of a property over time due to inflation, supply and demand, capital improvements and other factors. Most real estate investors purchase income property for cash flow and capital appreciation. It is important for real estate investors to understand the causes of value appreciation in order to make more profit-able investment decisions. Properties appreciate in value—or fail to appreciate--for many reasons. The seasoned real estate investor will look for a combi-nation of factors that will result in high appreciation growth rates.

3. Tax Benefits

Real estate can produce substantial tax savings that can transform a fair investment into a very good one. The goal is to protect large amounts of income from taxation. Deductions are available for most real estate investments. For instance, mort-gage loan interest can be deducted to offset an equal amount of income. Borrowing $50,000 at 9 percent interest will yield an interest deduction of $4,500 during the first year of the loan, which can be used to offset $4,500 of income that would ordi-narily be subject to income taxes. Regarding its ef-fect on taxes, the interest deduction for investment real estate is the same as the interest deduction for a home mortgage.

Property taxes levied against investment real estate and paid to state or local governments can also be deducted from taxable income. The deduction for property taxes you pay on investment real estate is treated in the same manner as the property taxes paid on your home, if you itemize deductions. The higher the property taxes you pay, the greater the tax savings you can realize.

Insurance premiums for coverage of real estate investments are deductible from taxable income. Insurance premiums are not deductible for owner occupants. Maintenance expenses are fully deductible in calculating your tax liability for a real estate investment. Expenses you incur for repairing rotting wood around a water heater or painting the deck are examples of costs that can be deducted from your other income, thus giving you a lower tax bill. Maintenance costs can be quite substantial, especially for older properties. Being able to deduct those expenses is a very important benefit of owning investment property, a benefit not available to homeowners. However, improvements that prolong the life or increase the value of the real estate are treated differently from maintenance costs. While maintenance expenses can be deducted in the year that they're incurred, improvement costs must be used to increase the cost basis of the real estate, thereby reducing any gain or increasing any loss when the property is eventually sold.

Depreciation accounts for the decline in value of an asset over time, including most real estate. Depreciation decreases the accounting value (the value of the property as shown on financial statements) of real estate and at the same time offsets an equal amount of income from taxation, yet does not affect the market value of the property. Investors generally obtain maximum tax benefits by depreciating real estate as quickly as possible. Rapid depreciation offsets income and saves taxes sooner. Residential rental property currently must be depreciated equally over twenty-seven and one-half years, while commercial investment property must be depreciated over thirty-nine years.

4. Leverage

Leverage is a powerful reason for investing in real estate. If an investor uses 100 percent cash to acquire a house worth $100,000, and the house increases in value by $5,000 in one year, then the investor has made a return of 5 percent (assuming no other costs). However, if the investor obtains 95 percent financing, only $5,000 cash would be required at the closing table, and a bank or other lender would lend the remaining $95,000 to buy the property. Assuming the same $5,000 increase in value, the investor's cash contribution of $5,000 would yield an increase in equity of $5,000 in one year, a 100 percent return. Leverage is a great way to maximize profits.

5. Flexibility

Investing in real estate is something that you can do part-time. Your investing does not have to interfere with your work or family life. If you do all the necessary preparation and make smart business decisions, you can build wealth over time without a major interruption in your current career.

Are ready to build wealth by investing in real estate? The next 30 days will be a lot of work, so you must be determined to buy your first property. You will be transformed from a student of real estate into a real estate investor. The next 30 days will go by so fast that it will seem instant. That is what you want, isn't it?

Let's get started!

CHAPTER 2

CLARIFY YOUR VISION

A man, to carry a successful business, must have imagination. He must see things as in a vision, a dream of the whole thing.

Charles M. Schwab

How long have you been waiting for something to happen? You work hard every day but you don't always see the fruits of your labor. You give more, dream big, but cannot get ahead. You feel like your life is a treadmill. You go, pick up speed along the way; however, when you look around you are in the same spot that you thought you were leaving. If you have a job, you desire more from your employer. If you have a business, you require more from your employees. In the end, you feel frustrated and defeated at times.

If you shook your head on any of these thoughts and were reminded of the pain that you hide from those around you, I am encouraged that you are reading this book. I must share a secret with you: what you are feeling is very common. One similarity among all human beings is that we want more and dream about a better future. The difference: Successful people act on those desires. Successful people live their dreams by taking needed actions to accomplish well thought-out, measurable goals. Others just daydream and wait for something to happen. These are the ordinary ones: those who want their lives to be different but are not consistent in acting in ways that are positive and progressive to change their situation. So, before you try this next endeavor, do some soul-searching. Assess your current state to see if you are capable of living a different future.

Are you really all that *unhappy* with the way things are? Are you searching for a feeling instead of a state of mind? These questions are important, because in order for you to thrive in your new future, you have to able to handle uncertainty, ridicule, and much discomfort. Any time a person experiences new situations that are difficult or unfamiliar, it is human nature to resort back to familiar patterns or an environment that is comfortable even when it is self-destructive.

Trying something new is challenging enough. But when you add the negative comments of friends and family along with self-doubt of wondering "should I be happy with what I have because I am really blessed," you may continue on your path to nowhere. I am sure you have done it countless times. You decide you really want to improve your fitness level, so one evening you start out on a brisk walk. Just as get into your stride you approach a steep hill. Your confidence and determination gets you up the first 200 feet of the incline. Halfway up, you feel the sweat dripping in your eyes, your heart is racing, and your shoes feel like they're glued to your feet. You can feel the calf muscles tightening and your arms struggling to swing to give you the momentum you need to keep going. This is the time that your mind tries to soothe your aching body. Your mind tells you that in this hot weather you can have a heart attack or nobody is watching so you can stop when you want or you can always just try again tomorrow. What you decide in that instant will determine whether you make it to the top of the hill where you will have a new sense of accomplishment. At the top of the hill, your view is a clear picture of how far you have come and the new-found strength you have to get you over the next hill. On the other hand, in that instant you could decide to remain at the bottom of the hill, where a lot of people attempt to make the climb but remain in the same spot for whatever reason holds them back.

Successful people have a vision. Forming and focusing upon a clear vision helps you choose which opportunities to pursue. A clear vision means you don't waste time on things that don't fit with your goals. Businesses have discovered the power of having a focused mission and vision statement. Many corporations now include a statement of core values as well. Vision-driven business owners have discovered that there is a good, bottom line reason for charting a direction. They are improving the odds that they will be successful. Having a vision will help you to choose among many paths and make faster progress toward your goals.

DAY 1

Define Your Mission

To develop your mission, look beyond the obvious things such as salary and benefits and ask yourself "Why do I work?" "What greater purpose do I serve?" That will help you determine your purpose- or mission. An example is, "To get satisfaction from helping young children experience success."

_____
_____
_____
_____
_____
_____
_____
_____
_____
_____
_____
_____
_____
_____
_____
_____
_____
_____
_____
_____
_____

Create Your Vision

A mission states the purpose of your career (the what and why) but your vision points to your destination (where you want to go) in the next three to ten years. To discover your long-term vision, imagine that you are at the end of your career looking back over the years. Ask yourself, "What did I want to accomplish?" "Where did I want to end up?" "What journey should I have taken, given the talents and abilities I have?"

Keep your vision short. Make it motivating and compelling. Use words that create a picture. For example, John Kennedy's: "Put a man on the moon by the end of the decade." An educator's: "Be the teacher that every student will remember as an adult." Bill Gates, Microsoft: "Put a computer on every desk in America."

_____

_____

_____

_____

_____

_____

_____

_____

_____

_____

_____

_____

_____

Define Your Values

You may also want to put your core values down on paper. These values describe the beliefs that guide every action you take. Some examples could be: Treat all people with respect. Act with honesty and integrity.

Here are some common values

Achievement	Challenge	Wealth
Freedom	Honesty	Independence
Leadership	Morality/Ethics	Power
Recognition	Self-Respect	Security
Trust	Wisdom	Integrity
Creativity	Comfort	Loyalty
Risk	Personal development	Faith

Develop a Statement on your Core Values

_____

_____

_____

_____

_____

_____

_____

_____

_____

_____

_____

_____

_____

_____

_____

_____

_____

_____

_____

_____

_____

_____

_____

_____

_____

_____

Check the parts of your life you want to change/improve:

☐ Spiritual life

☐ Personal development

☐ Leisure time

☐ Professional

☐ Civic/community

☐ Family

☐ Social

☐ Health/physical well-being

☐ Education

☐ Finances

☐ Other _____

☐ Other _____

What is hold me back from improving each one?

1. _____
_____
_____

2. _____
_____
_____

3. _____
_____
_____

4. _____
_____
_____

5. _____
_____
_____

DAY 2

Define the dreams for your life

1. _____
   _____
   _____

2. _____
   _____
   _____

3. _____
   _____
   _____

4. _____
   _____
   _____

5. _____
   _____
   _____

What sacrifices are you willing to make to accomplish your dreams?

1. _____
   _____
   _____

2. _____
   _____
   _____

3. _____
   _____
   _____

4. _____
   _____
   _____

5. _____
   _____
   _____

If you do not live the life of your dreams, what impact will this have on you and the people most important to you?

_____

_____

_____

_____

Will I live the life of my dreams by becoming a real estate investor?

Yes or No

If Yes, How?

_____

_____

_____

What actions will I take immediately to become a real estate investor?

_____

_____

_____

_____

_____

What actions will I take to maintain a positive mental attitude as I learn the business?

_____

_____

_____

_____

_____

I will seek the following people to hold me accountable:

My real estate investing coach is

_____

_____

My real estate investing mentor is

_____

_____

My business coach or consultant is

_____

_____

CHAPTER 3

DO YOUR RESEARCH

Before anything else, preparation is the key to success.

Alexander Graham Bell

Everyone has seen the chef on television preparing a meal before an audience. He has all of the ingredients laid out premeasured and organized in the order he will use them to prepare a meal that everyone is salivating and anticipating to taste. The next five days will be equivalent to this concept. First you will prepare your office to conduct your business. The next four days will be used to research the areas you will focus to acquire your properties. Eventually, you will be the expert in the zip codes that you invest, but you must do your due diligence by using the resources that is available to acquire this information. You will need to purchase a large area map to get a good visual of the zip codes of the city and outlying areas. Eventually, you place stickpins in the areas you have houses.

It is my suggestion that you begin in the neighborhood that you live. On the other hand, if you don't live in a neighborhood that does not offer many homes that would be ideal for the rental market. For instance, if you in a multi-million dollar home with very wealthy neighbors, I do not suggest you start in your neighborhood. I also don't suggest that you focus on a deteriorating area with high crime and drug activity. Choose five zip codes to start your research. You will eliminate two in the next few days based on your research. Start analyzing properties with three areas of focus and remember that you have years to become an expert in many areas. For now, let's keep it simple.

DAY 3

Create a Productive Environment

Now it is time to set up your office. You are starting a business so it is important to have a space so that you can study in order to grow your business. If you do not have a home office, turn a spare room into your office. No matter what room you choose, it should be free from distractions like video games, television, children, etc. Be sure to set up boundaries with your family and friends to let them know you are working on your business when you are in your office.

First things first, buy your list of office supplies and get organized. Next, use your calendar to allocate 2-4 hours over the next 30 days to work in your business. You will probably need to devote more hours on the weekends.

List of office supplies and equipment

Computer	Stick Pins
High speed internet	Paper Clips
Phone	Stapler
Paper	5 Binders
Pens	Tabs
Highlighters	Filing Folders
Scissors	Filing Bin
Calculator	Large map of the city
Tape	Cork Board
Calendar	GPS system

Create a Vision Board also called a Dream Board

1. Go through magazines and tear out images, pictures, words, or headlines that portray your vision

2. Organize in categories (Family, Career, Wealth, Toys, Health)

3. Tape a picture of yourself in the middle

4. Stick or tape images on the cork board with each corner designated for a category

5. Hang the board in a place where you can see it often

Be creative and believe in your vision

DAY 4

Research Your Local Market

Five Zip Codes to Research

1. _____

2. _____

3. _____

4. _____

5. _____

Collect demographic information on the zip codes from any of these sources:

- Public records or tax assessor's office

- www.Zipskinny.com

- www.FreeDemographicsData.com

- www.Zipwho.com

Check retail pricing from free online sources such as

- www.Trulia.com

- www.Zillow.com

- www.mls.com

There are many online resources. The ones I have suggested are just a few that are available.

Analyze your data

Zip Code	Pros	Cons
1.		
2.		
3.		
4.		
5.		

☐ **Eliminate one zip code** _____

DAY 5

Go For A Drive

1. Fill your gas tank and go for a drive through your top four zip codes

2. Observe the neighborhoods and make notes on your observations

   o Is there development or new construction?

   o Are the homes and yards well kept and mani-cured?

   o Are there abandoned properties?

   o Are houses vacant or boarded up?

   o If there are friendly people walking, ask them about their neighborhood.

   o Make notes based on your observations

Zip Code	Pros	Cons
1.		
2.		
3.		
4.		

Based on your observations and your personal criteria for the areas you want to invest, eliminate one zip code.

Eliminated zip code: _____

DAY 6

Make Phone Calls

☐ Call 3-5 real estate agents in your area. They can be found in ads from the paper or online, referrals from friends, or from signs when you are driving around town. Inquire if they are real estate investors or have experience working with numerous investors. This question is key because if they don't understand the real estate investment business, it is going to be difficult for them to think outside the box of traditional real estate and eventually will be a waste of your time. You want an agent who can walk into a house that smells and needs of lots of repairs, see beyond cosmetic work, and help you work the numbers for profit. You want to do this over and over again. If they sound confused when you say real estate investor and starts pushing a new home for the perfect family, hang up! Trust me on this one.

☐ Choose 2-3 that are knowledgeable in real estate investing and ask them to start sending you lists of properties in your top 4 zip codes. Also ask them their opinions of those zip codes.

☐ Call 2-3 Accounts and have the same criteria I discussed for real estate agents. Choose one to work with and make an appointment to set up your business entity. Later this accountant will be the one who does all the tedious work for your tax return. If the accountant is a real estate investor, ask his opinion on the four zip codes you have chosen.

☐ Call a few real estate investors you already know and get their opinion of your four zip codes.

☐ Based on information you have received from those already in the business and your personal criteria, eliminate one zip code.

Eliminated Zip Code: _____

DAY 7

Chose Your Area

3 Zip Codes of Focus

1. _____

2. _____

3. _____

☐ Make a folder for each zip code to organize property information

CHAPTER 4

WHERE IS THE MONEY?

Empty pockets never held anyone back.
Only empty heads and empty hearts can do that.

Norman Vincent Peale

In the next few days you will work diligently to gather all your financial statements, create a budget, and begin to process how you finance your deals depending on your particular financial situation. Real estate investors can have poor credit, low or no income, or both. Don't be discouraged about your situation. I challenge you to start working on your particular issues and continue to change your mindset. Begin to think creatively in order to accomplish your goal—acquiring real estate. This goal may not fall into the traditional ways of purchasing real estate.

Traditional ways of purchasing residential real estate are most common for, and work well for, the kinds of homes in which you want to live, raise a family, and grow old. But you are now in the real estate business—keyword: *business*—and traditional financing may not work. Indeed, for a large percentage of residential real estate investors, traditional financing simply *won't* work. As you become more experienced, you'll learn that traditional modes of financing are, in the real estate investment business, actually quite uncommon. Right now, though,

I simply want you to keep an open mind and preserve all of your financing options—including some that may not ever have occurred to you!

You've likely begun with this question: Where am I going to get the money? It's a common question, and a natural one. The money is there, I can assure you—somewhere. You just have to know how to find it. But before we look at finding someone else's money to finance your purchase—certainly my favorite kind of money! —Let's take a clear, honest look at you and your money.

DAY 8

Gather Personal Documents

Today you will gather all of your personal documents for several reasons:

- Gain a snapshot of your financial situation

- Create a financial statement

- Create a monthly budget

- Complete your bank book

- Decide on your financing options.

Step 1

Please check off the following tasks as you complete them.

__ Gather your last two years' tax returns (full return if you itemized deductions)

__ Check stubs or salary statements of the last two pay periods

__ Bank statements from all checking and savings accounts

__ Investment statements: CD's, stocks, bonds, retirement accounts, Investment Retirement Accounts (IRAs), mutual funds, money market accounts

__ Information on any assets that you own: land, property, boats, cars, trust funds, jewelry, etc

Step 2

Using two sheets of paper, write assets on one and liabilities on the other

___ On the assets page, list all cash from checking, savings, CDs, and money market accounts, retirement accounts as well as the value of any property you own

___ On the liabilities page, list everything you owe money such as house, car, credit cards, all loans, notes, etc.

Step 3

Create your financial statement by entering the information in a spreadsheet to calculate your net worth.

PERSONAL FINANCIAL STATEMENT

Name
Date

Assets	Amount in Dollars
Cash - checking accounts	$-
Cash - savings accounts	-
Certificates of deposit	-
Securities - stocks / bonds / mutual funds	-
Notes & contracts receivable	-
Life insurance *(cash surrender value)*	-
Personal property *(autos, jewelry, etc.)*	-
Retirement Funds *(eg. IRAs, 401k)*	-
Real estate *(market value)*	-
Other assets *(specify)*	-
Other assets *(specify)*	-
Total Assets	**$-**

Liabilities	Amount in Dollars
Current Debt *(Credit cards, Accounts)*	$-
Notes payable *(describe below)*	-
Taxes payable	-
Real estate mortgages *(describe)*	-
Other liabilities *(specify)*	-
Other liabilities *(specify)*	-
Total Liabilities	**$-**
Net Worth	**$-**

Signature: **Date:**

Download document from www.jumpstartrealestateinvesting.com

DAY 9

Create A Budget

I don't know too many people who like even to create a budget, let alone follow one month after month. Most Americans in fact are caught in a paycheck-to-paycheck existence, doing much more spending than saving, and planning neither. You, as a beginner real estate investor, are embarking on a business venture. An unplanned business is a plan for failure. And an unbudgeted business is a *guaranteed* failure. The message—one I cannot put too strongly: You *must* draft a sensible budget… you *must* use that budget and live by it…you *must* review and revise that budget as you move along.

Don't think of budgeting *just* as a chore, however, budgeting is very much a freeing thing, psychologically. Many people fail to budget primarily because they don't want to face facts or fears. Oftentimes, though, you'll be surprised, in the budgeting process, by discovering possible sources of income you hadn't seen before, and by remembering or rediscovering assets you hadn't thought about. Almost universally, in applying their minds to a budget, people find new ways of eliminating expenses, new ideas for shedding some of the enormous loads of "stuff" most of us carry, new ways of making money or spending less. Starting the budgeting process can be daunting. Finishing a good basic budget, however, is usually very much a hopeful, uplifting experience.

1. Gather bank statements, credit card statements, monthly bills, and paychecks—you used them yesterday to create your financial statement.

2. Using the monthly budget worksheet, record all sources of income that includes fixed and variable expenses.

3. Calculate totals and make adjustments in expenses if your expenses are overextended.

Sample Budget

Personal Monthly Budget

PROJECTED MONTHLY INCOME	Income 1		4,300.00
	Extra income		300.00
	Total monthly income		**4,600.00**

ACTUAL MONTHLY INCOME	Income 1		4,000.00
	Extra income		300.00
	Total monthly income		**4,300.00**

PROJECTED BALANCE (Projected income minus expenses)	**3,405.00**
ACTUAL BALANCE (Actual income minus expenses)	**3,064.00**
DIFFERENCE (Actual minus projected)	**(341.00)**

HOUSING	Projected Cost	Actual Cost	Difference
Mortgage or rent	1,000.00	1,000.00	0.00
Phone	54.00	100.00	(46.00)
Electricity	44.00	56.00	(12.00)
Gas	22.00	28.00	(6.00)
Water and sewer	8.00	8.00	0.00
Cable	34.00	34.00	0.00
Waste removal	10.00	10.00	0.00
Maintenance or repairs	23.00	0.00	23.00
Supplies	0.00	0.00	0.00
Other	0.00	0.00	0.00
Subtotals	1,195.00	1,236.00	(41.00)

TRANSPORTATION	Projected Cost	Actual Cost	Difference
Vehicle payment			0.00
Bus/taxi fare			0.00
Insurance			0.00
Licensing			0.00
Fuel			0.00
Maintenance			0.00
Other			0.00
Subtotals	0.00	0.00	0.00

INSURANCE	Projected Cost	Actual Cost	Difference
Home			0.00
Health			0.00
Life			0.00
Other			0.00
Subtotals	0.00	0.00	0.00

FOOD	Projected Cost	Actual Cost	Difference
Groceries			0.00
Dining out			0.00
Other			0.00
Subtotals	0.00	0.00	0.00

PETS	Projected Cost	Actual Cost	Difference
Food			0.00
Medical			0.00
Grooming			0.00
Toys			0.00
Other			0.00
Subtotals	0.00	0.00	0.00

PERSONAL CARE	Projected Cost	Actual Cost	Difference
Medical			0.00
Hair/nails			0.00
Clothing			0.00
Dry cleaning			0.00
Health club			0.00
Organization dues or fees			0.00
Other			0.00
Subtotals	0.00	0.00	0.00

ENTERTAINMENT	Projected Cost	Actual Cost	Difference
Video/DVD			0.00
CDs			0.00
Movies			0.00
Concerts			0.00
Sporting events			0.00
Live theater			0.00
Other			0.00
Other			0.00
Other			0.00
Subtotals	0.00	0.00	0.00

LOANS	Projected Cost	Actual Cost	Difference
Personal			0.00
Student			0.00
Credit card			0.00
Credit card			0.00
Credit card			0.00
Other			0.00
Subtotals	0.00	0.00	0.00

TAXES	Projected Cost	Actual Cost	Difference
Federal			0.00
State			0.00
Local			0.00
Other			0.00
Subtotals	0.00	0.00	0.00

SAVINGS OR INVESTMENTS	Projected Cost	Actual Cost	Difference
Retirement account			0.00
Investment account			0.00
Other			0.00
Subtotals	0.00	0.00	0.00

GIFTS AND DONATIONS	Projected Cost	Actual Cost	Difference
Charity 1			0.00
Charity 2			0.00
Charity 3			0.00
Subtotals	0.00	0.00	0.00

LEGAL	Projected Cost	Actual Cost	Difference
Attorney			0.00
Alimony			0.00
Payments on lien or judgment			0.00
Other			0.00
Subtotals	0.00	0.00	0.00

TOTAL PROJECTED COST	**1,195.00**
TOTAL ACTUAL COST	**1,236.00**
TOTAL DIFFERENCE	**(41.00)**

DAY 10
Study Common Real Estate Terms

As you become an experienced real estate investor, you will become more familiar with real estate terms that investors use. I have listed the most common ones for you to learn so that you can communicate like a professional real estate investor.

Bird dog—someone who identifies a potentially good real estate investment opportunity and passes that deal on to another investor for a fee.

Capitalization (Cap) rate—the rate at which you discount future income to determine its present value:

Cap rate = Net operating income / Value

Cash flow—net operating income minus the total debt service payments.

Cash-on-cash return—cash flow (usually before taxes) from a particular year of a property's operation and compared to the cash you invested to purchase the property, expressed as a percentage:

Cash-on-Cash Return = Cash Flow / Cash Investment

Cash out—the cash given to the borrower from the proceeds of a loan

Creative **financing**—any financing arrangement other than a traditional mortgage from a third-party lending institution.

Earnest money—a deposit made by a purchaser of real estate to show good faith.

Hard money loan—a loan that is underwritten with the condition and value of the property as primary criteria for approval. These loans are usually approved within days and funded in less than two weeks. The cost of for the benefits of speed in funding and lax underwriting is typically a moderate to high interest rate.

Lease option—a lease combined with an option agreement conveying the right to purchase the property under specified conditions.

Lease purchase—a lease combined with a purchase agreement that obliges the tenant to purchase the property under specified conditions.

Real estate owned (REO) property—property acquired by a lender through foreclosure and held in the lender's inventory.

Seasoning—a loan which has been in force for a period of time, typically six months or more, thus establishing borrower's payment history.

Wholesale—to contract a property with the intention of reselling it quickly at a higher price.

These are just a few common terms to get you started. The glossary contains other terms that you can access as needed.

DAY 11
Analyze Financing Options

As you prepare to acquire your first deal, it is essential that you begin to plan how you will finance the property you decide to purchase first. Next, I will discuss some options for you to consider. The options are divided between your own and other people's money (OPM).

Your Own Money	Other People's Money (OPM)
Equity lines of credit	Bank loan
Credit cards	Private investor
Cash value in life insurance	Commercial lines of credit
Self-directed IRA	Seller financing
Second mortgage	Assumable loans and mortgages
Cash from savings	
Cash from checking account	
CDs, bonds, or stocks	

1. Analyze your personal financial statement and your monthly budget to decide how much you have to commit in your new business or have access to as collateral when you seek financing. Fill in the following blanks.

Liquid Assets (Cash from Checking, Savings, Money Market) = _____

2. Research the different options in the OPM column. You can find this information online, your local banking institution, or an experienced real estate investor. After you have gathered your information, decide the three options you will seek immediately.

My three options:

1. _____

2. _____

3. _____

DAY 12

Get Pre-Approved

Yesterday, you explored different financing options. Today, you will gain more clarity on the direction you need to take, because you will seek pre-approval for a mortgage loan. You will go to the bank or credit union with which you already have a relationship (via your checking, savings, CD, or money market account). Explain to your banker that you will be buying a property soon and would like to get preapproved so that you will know what you can afford. The results will give you an idea on how "bankable" you are so that you can develop a well thought-out strategy on how you will acquire your investment properties.

Pre-approval checklist

__ Bank Application for Pre-Approval Submitted

__ Results from Pre-Approval: Great—Good—Fair—Needs Improvement

__ Maximum Loan Amount _____

__ Copy of Pre-Approval certificate

DAY 13

Organize Your Presentation Binder

I am sure you have heard the admonition *Never judge a book by its cover*. Wise as this advice may be, the truth is that many people will judge you in the first minute by how you look, walk, and talk. For this reason, I encourage you to look professional at all times as you build your business in real estate investing. Today, however, you will focus in particular on how you present *when asking for money*.

You would be amazed at the stories I have heard from lenders who described "wanna-be" investors who have walked into their offices asking for thousands of dollars without a business plan, without a plan at all! My experience has been very positive when I have gone to potential lenders with my presentation binder. I gave the impression that I was a business owner with a solid plan because I had *proof*. Several times I have heard remarks such as *I've never seen anything like this...I wish more people would come in with something like this* and *This is really impressive!*

Your presentation binder is a simple book that will produce huge results. In the beginning, it will not have as much in it, and some tabs maybe empty. However, it will become fuller as you become experienced and grow your business. The tools you will need are the following:

1. 3-ring binder (half-inch or 1-inch)

2. Cover sheet

3. Divider tab sets with 8 tabs.

I suggest the following arrangement for your divider tabs...

TAB 1	**Business Plan**
TAB 2	**Personal Financial Statement**
TAB 3	**Tax Returns**—last two years tax return
TAB 4	**My Business Team**—names and contact information for your team
TAB 5	**Properties**—pictures and cash flow analyses of the properties you will add to your portfolio
TAB 6	**References**—letters of support from credible people you know well
TAB 7	**Miscellaneous Information**—this could include your resume or, lists of workshops or seminars you have attended on real estate investing, professional and community and other organizations to which you belong, and other information which may support your credibility and your status as a responsible investor and desirable member of the business community.
TAB 8	**Credit Report**---copy of most recent credit report

DAY 14

Create Your Financing Roadmap

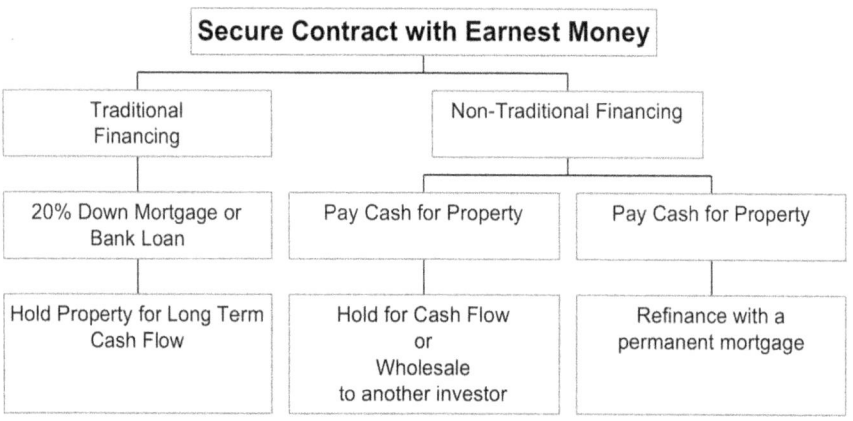

Determine the best route for your situation and your real estate investing goals

_____

_____

_____

_____

CHAPTER 5

IT'S NOT PERSONAL, IT'S BUSINESS

Create a definite plan for carrying out your desire and begin at once, whether you are ready or not, to put this plan into action.

Napoleon Hill

Let's be serious. Real Estate investing is not a hobby—it's a *business*. So the next few days will be spent making a decision on the best legal form or entity to build your empire upon and to complete your business plan. I know these are daunting tasks, but they are essential.

Here is a brief description of the major kinds of business entities that can be used to conduct a real estate investment business…

Sole Proprietorship

The sole proprietorship is owned and run by one individual. In the sole proprietorship, there is no legal distinction between the owner and the business. All profits and all losses accrue to the owner (subject to taxation). The owner owns directly all the assets of the business, and all debts of the business are his debts—he must pay them from his personal resources. This means that the owner has unlimited liability. This is a "sole" proprietorship in the sense that the owner has no partners. A sole proprietor may do business using a trade name other than his or her legal name. This also allows the proprietor to open a business account with banking institutions.

Some advantages of a sole proprietorship are that this form of business offers

- Easier start-up than most other forms

- Mode of operation subject to fewer regulations than are other types of businesses

- Full autonomy to the owner with regard to business decisions

- Easier discontinuance.

Another major advantage of the sole proprietorship is that the proprietor, as an individual, takes all the profits of the business. A sole proprietorship is not a corporation—it does not pay corporate taxes. Rather, the person who organized the business pays self-employment taxes on the profits made, making tax filing much simpler. A sole proprietorship also does not have to be concerned with double taxation, as a corporate entity would. A sole proprietor usually has a quick decision process and doesn't face any opposition when making a decision, as he or she has total control of his or her business. All profits and losses accrue to the owner. The owner does not have to be concerned with the tension and conflict attendant to partnership, as there are no partners. The sole proprietorship is one of the easiest types of business to start, with little paperwork and only small costs involved in set-up.

A major disadvantage of a sole proprietorship is that the owner has unlimited liability, as he is responsible for the business's debts because he has control over the business. If the business becomes successful, the risks accompanying the business tend to grow. To minimize those risks, a sole proprietor has the option of forming a corporation or a limited liability company.

Partnership

The partnership is a business entity ordinarily comprised of two or more individuals, although under some circumstances a partnership will be formed between other kinds of business entities, or between individuals and one or more other business entities. The partnership is relatively inexpensive and simple to create and maintain, but poses tax and liability issues that are similar to those encountered in a sole proprietorship.

While a written partnership agreement is not ordinarily required as a matter of law, it is always a good idea for partners to formalize their business relationship in writing. The partnership agreement should specify, among other things, the business name, the official business address, the identities of the partners, and how profits are to be divided among the partners. The agreement should also reflect each partner's contribution to the partnership, the value of that contribution, and the resulting ownership interest. If you do not intend the partners to have equal management duties and decision-making authority, the partnership agreement should indicate the duties and authority granted to each partner.

The partnership agreement may also specify what happens if you wish to bring in a new partner, if a partner decides to leave or wishes to be bought out, and what happens if the other partners wish to eject or buy out a partner, including a formula for valuing the partner's share. Many partnerships encounter significant difficulties when a partner dies or wishes to quit, and there is no agreed-upon formula for determining the amount the other partners must pay to buy out that partner's interest. You may also wish to specify a method of resolution of disputes between partners, such as mediation or arbitration, so as to keep partnership disputes out of court.

There are significant liability issues raised by partnership. Ordinarily, a partner is individually liable not only for business debts and liabilities, but also for most business-related conduct of the other partners. For example, in a law firm partnership where one partner commits an act of legal malpractice, all of the other partners will ordinarily be personally liable for any resultant damages awarded, and their personal assets will be subject to seizure to cover that award. That is to say, for purposes of liability, the acts of one partner are attributed to all of the other partners.

Similarly, if one partner binds the partnership into a business arrangement or contract, all the other partners are bound by that action. For instance, if a partner goes out and leases office space or takes out a loan in the name of the partnership—even if the other partners don't feel that they were properly consulted or that it was a wise business move— the partnership will ordinarily remain liable for the payments, and if the partnership fails to make payments the other partners may be personally liable.

Most partnerships take the form of a **general partnership**, where all partners have some management authority. Another option is to create a **limited partnership**, where there are "general partners" who direct the business of the partnership and "limited partners" who have no management role. The general partner may be another kind of business entity, such as a corporation or LLC. Limited partnership is often used for real estate transactions, where investors sign on as limited partners, and the general partner manages the property. Limited partners have little or no role in the management of the business. In return for surrendering that authority, their responsibility for business debts and liabilities is limited to the amount of their investment. Due to the complicated laws and regulations governing limited partnerships, I highly recommend that you work with an attorney.

Limited Liability Company

A limited liability company, or LLC, is a business entity that carries many of the advantages of a corporation, while avoiding many of the burdens imposed on corporations, and while retaining many of the characteristics of unincorporated entities such as partnerships and sole proprietorships. While the owners of a corporation are referenced as shareholders or stockholders, the owners of a limited liability company are often referenced as "members." It is possible for an LLC to be formed by a single individual, in which case it is usually referenced as a "single-member LLC."

Members of a limited liability company enjoy protection from individual liability similar to that afforded to corporate shareholders. That is to say, if a business is sued or is unable to pay its debts, the creditors can ordinarily only reach the LLC's assets and cannot reach the assets of the members. While in most states the law is not yet developed, some states do permit an action to "pierce the corporate veil" of an LLC and reach the personal assets of members who have engaged in wrongful conduct. Whatever the current law in any given jurisdiction, owners of an LLC should anticipate that, if they use the LLC to advance their personal purposes or to perpetrate fraud, courts would hold them personally liable for the LLC's associated liabilities. Also, individuals can be held responsible for their own negligence and misconduct, for actions intended to damage or defraud the LLC, and for debts of the LLC that they have personally guaranteed.

When starting an LLC, you must prepare Articles of Organization, these to be filed with the Secretary of State along with a filing fee. Most states offer approved forms for completing and submitting articles of organization. Typically, the Articles of Organization include the name and address of the LLC, the names and addresses of the initial members (owners), and the name and address of the LLC's in state registered agent. Regulations, forms, the labels given to various documents, and incorporation fees do vary from one jurisdiction to another, but the limited information given here does in general terms describe the pattern in typical U.S. jurisdictions.

When starting an LLC, though generally not required by law, members should create and approve an operating agreement for the LLC. The operating agreement governs the operation and management systems for the LLC, and can direct the manner in which profits are to be divided. It can also create procedures for the departure of LLC members, or the addition of new members, and the valuation of the LLC for purposes of buy-in or buy-out. The agreement should also reflect the ownership interests of the members, their associated voting rights, and how profits are to be distributed among the owners. Without an operating agreement, state law—which may not be advantageous to the LLC or the business it conducts—will govern the basic operation of the LLC. Unlike corporations, LLCs are not required to hold annual meetings or prepare annual reports. It is helpful to have an attorney review the proposed final version of an LLC's operating agreement prior to its formal adoption. Some states require that LLCs pay an annual franchise tax or registration fee.

Corporations

A corporation is a business entity created under state law, an entity that stands as an independent legal "person" apart from its shareholders and directors. A corporation's owners or shareholders receive the benefit of limited liability for the obligations of the corporation, and are thus ordinarily shielded from the corporation's creditors, even in the event the corporation cannot pay its obligations. There are procedural requirements imposed on corporations, which may deter some businesses from opting to incorporate. Once again, you are strongly urged to consult a duly qualified lawyer in your jurisdiction before making any final decisions about a corporate structure you will use or any binding agreement you will enter into with other individuals or business entities.

'C' Corporation

This and the next section describe two major categories of corporation—the 'C' corporation and the 'S' corporation.

A corporation is treated, under law, as a 'C' Corporation unless it specifically elects to be treated as an 'S' Corporation. The C Corporation may become a public corporation, with its shares being bought and sold as stock. It may ordinarily deduct the entire value of the fringe benefits offered to shareholders, who also serve as employees. There is no limit on the number of shareholders, and people who are neither citizens nor residents of the United

States may hold shares. Advantages to the C Corporation include its flexibility to carry corporate losses forward to future tax years. In some circumstances, corporate profits will be subject to "double taxation," first as corporate income and second as income to the ultimate recipient. For example, if a corporation issues dividends from its profits, it has already paid income tax on that money, but the dividends are taxable as income to the shareholders. The C Corporation cannot pass losses through to investors.

'S' Corporation

An S Corporation elects to have its profits pass through to its shareholders. The shareholders of an S Corporation receive the benefit of limited liability, and are treated in the manner of partners for purposes of taxation. S Corporation cannot have more than 75 shareholders, all of whom must be individuals, estates, or qualifying trusts. Other qualifications include these:

- S Corporation must have only one class of stock

- S Corporation must be formed in the United States

- All shareholders must be citizens or legal residents of the U.S.

Profits are generally not potentially subject to double-taxation, first as corporate profits and second as personal income when distributed to the shareholders. Thus, when choosing between an 'S' Corporation and a 'C' Corporation, stockholders should consider the impact of paying taxes at the corporate rate as distinct from their personal marginal tax rates. You should discuss the full financial and tax benefits and consequences of 'S' Corporation status with your accountant, prior to making your choice.

The shareholders of an 'S' Corporation are limited in the amount they can deduct as a result of business losses, in rough terms, to the amount of their "basis" or investment in the corporation.

As you formalize your business plan, you will start to take yourself even more seriously in this new venture. As you analyze the different possible business entities available to you—sole proprietor, partnership, the different forms of corporation—and start researching your market, you'll feel a transformation taking place within you. You will start to *believe in yourself*. You may find that belief fleeting, however, as your old friend *fear* calls to ask: *Are you crazy?* Rude or not, please do hang up in his face. We'll deal with him later. Till then, stay on track and complete your tasks!

Take a deep breath, exhale, and let's carry on.....

DAY 15

Consult With An Accountant

You have learned that there are several forms of business. Now it's time to figure out which one is best for you. An accountant should guide you through the process. If you do not have an accountant, you can always look in the yellow pages or Google. My suggestion, however: Ask a business owner or another real estate investor to refer you to an accountant. If all else fails, every state has a State Board of Accountants, or you can search the American Institute of Certified Public Accountants.

When you've found an accountant, make an appointment to meet with her to see whether she is the best fit for you and your business. Share your business goals with her so that she can advise you on which is the best legal form for your business. Here are some more questions you want to ask when you meet with your accountant:

- How are you going to help my business grow?

- Are you a tax planner or a tax preparer?

- What benchmarks will you help me set for my business, so I can track my projects?

- Will you have to print my documents or will they be transferred electronically?

- What kind of accounting-related software will I need to buy?

- What other services do you offer? Estate planning, gift planning, legal referrals?

- Do you work with other real estate investors? How many?

Your accountant should be the financial quarterback for your business. Your business accountant should be more than just a tax preparer. He should be a strategist, a tax planner who will help you take advantage of business and tax laws during the business year. So, during your initial consultation, ask plenty of questions and take advantage of his expertise. Determine whether this person is a good fit for you and the best person for your team.

DAY 16

Form Your Business

Once you make a decision on your accountant— a matter that may take meeting with several candidates—she should file the necessary paperwork to form your business. Make several copies of your documents for your files, your presentation binder, and your business plan. Of course the question of which business entity you'll use is never just an accounting or tax issue—it's often a legal issue as well. Be sure you consult both a well qualified accountant and an appropriately qualified attorney for purposes of helping you choose your form of business and drafting the necessary documents.

FINAL CHECKLIST

Items to Be Completed	Check if Completed
Choose & Register a Business Name	
Decide on the Legal Form for the Business	
Write a Business Plan	
Set Up a Relationship with a Banker	
Set Up a Relationship with an Attorney	
Meet Legal Requirements for Operating a Business	
Get Licenses and Permits	
Plan for Risk with Liability Insurance	
Set up Recordkeeping Systems	
Set up a Financial Management System	

DAY 17

Define Your Team

Developing a real estate investing team may be the most important key to the success of your investment. Henry Ford was famous for saying he did not know all the answers, but knew where to find them. An investment team is no different. You don't have to know all the real estate answers—just know where to find them. A great investment team will even think of questions you never knew to ask!

Some basic team members come to mind when getting started...

Attorney. While there are many different types of attorneys who practice in the real estate investment fields, two kinds in particular come to mind. First is your general closing attorney. She should be well versed in understanding titles, protecting you from fraudulent transactions, and good at getting paperwork filed in a timely manner. Your lawyer should also offer a reasonable fee for reviewing and drafting documents, and be available for questions.

The second type of attorney is one who focuses on landlord/tenant law. He will handle evictions, collections, application and lease drafting, and a number of other issues that may arise out of the management of property. He should be readily available for questions and advice. The more you talk to him initially, the less you will see him later.

CPA (Certified Public Accountant). Once you begin to create income, it is important you solicit the help of a professional who understands both federal and state income taxes and understands them, particularly, as they pertain to real estate. Because our business is ever evolving, you need an accountant who stays current on issues and advantages that you can capitalize on as your business grows. Much as with an attorney, it is never best to search for the cheapest. A good accountant should save you more in the long run than the fees charged you.

Mentor. It is always cheaper to learn from the mistakes of others than to make them yourself. A good mentor should be one with "fruit-on-the-tree" knowledge of the local real estate business. No matter what, a good mentor is someone interested in *your* success.

While there are a number of other people you could usefully add your team, including real estate agents, real estate professionals, and property management companies, I would consider these three essential to beginning the process.

As you search out people to fill these roles, it is important that they model some key attributes for a successful relationship. They should possess similar values. What good does a team member do you if you aren't working from the same set of values? Never work with someone you can't trust to do the right thing no matter the circumstance. People with set value systems consistently make better decisions.

Avoid yes-men. Your team should not agree with you all the time. This sounds like I'm saying the opposite of what I said before. Consider, however...if a team member agrees with you all the time, then one of you is useless. If you disagree all the time, then *both* of you are useless! Find someone who challenges your current investment thinking. Great team members will complement each other's skills.

A good team relationship is a win-win relationship. John Maxwell, leadership expert and author, says that if the other person is getting the best of the relationship, you need to figure out a way to give more to that relationship. If you feel that you are getting the raw end of the relationship deal, you need to dissolve the relationship. It is essential for both parties to profit from any successful relationship.

Developing an investment team is *essential* to your success. *Don't* go it alone. While you will never be able to eliminate the learning curve in any business, you can make it a much easier ride if you put the right people in the right positions on your team. Teamwork makes the dream work!

My Team Checklist

☐ Attorney

_____

☐ CPA

_____

☐ Mentor

_____

☐ Banker

_____

☐ Mortgage Broker

_____

☐ Private Lender

_____

☐ Real Estate Agent

_____

☐ Property Manager

_____

☐ Insurance Agent

_____

☐ Landscaper

_____

☐ General Contractor

_____

☐ Handy Man

_____

☐ Electrician

_____

DAY 18

Start Your Business Plan

Business can be as unpredictable as the waves in the sea. However, if you have a plan, you will be able to prepare yourself for the ups and downs. A business plan is your plan of action to help you communicate to others who will join you to know what the purpose of the business is. Your business plan will also serve as a tool by which you will convince lenders that your business idea is a feasible and marketable one. Writing a business plan allows you, the investor, to determine your real estate objectives. You will develop the road map for starting or expanding a successful business. Your plan can be used to obtain start-up capital or expansion financing.

Business plans can save you the trouble of pursuing a futile venture because they are designed to help you analyze your business idea. Your real estate business plan is intended to provide insight for developing and expanding your company. It is not written in stone. Review your business plan at least three to four times a year to ensure that you are on track.

In order to complete your basic written business plan, you will be conducting quite a bit of research. Don't let this discourage you, because we are going to keep it simple. Also writing a business plan can seem like an overwhelming task, so we will break it into sections to make it manageable.

As you create this new document, I will walk you, step by step, through each heading of your business plan.

1. Executive summary

This is usually the first thing investors, lenders, and potential business partners will read. It should be concise, containing all the information needed to grab your reader's attention of while summarizing the overall plan. Write this section *last*, I suggest.

Tips for writing the executive summary...

Keep you executive summary to two pages or less. Note that some readers even prefer executive summaries to paragraph length. If your executive summary runs to longer length—more than a page—consider preceding it with an even tighter one-paragraph summary, perhaps titled *Overview* or *In a nutshell*...

Keep each topic brief. Keep all topics at similar length—don't let one be hugely shorter or longer than the other, in your executive summary, even if you cover different topics at drastically different lengths in the body of your business plan.

Explain the fundamentals of your business: Who will be your customers? What do you think the future holds for your business and the real estate industry? Use bullets, charts, and graphs to highlight the most important information

2. Company description

- Mission statement: brief statement in 30 words or less that explains your reason for being and your guiding principles.

- Name and location of the company

- Who owns the company and its legal status (sole proprietor, partnership, LLC, 'C' or 'S' corporation)

- Description of your product or service

- Current real estate trends

- How is the company funded to date? If you are looking for funding, how much?

3. Products and Services

- Provide a detailed explanation of the products and services offered through your real estate business. Do you buy homes in a niche market (mobile homes, Section 8 rentals, etc)? Can you guide people through difficult situations such as bankruptcy, foreclosure, or short sales?

- What factors will give you a competitive advantage?

4. Market Analysis

It is imperative to research your market and industry. The good news is that there are websites you can use to gather information at no cost:

www.census.gov—all U.S. census data with information about people, businesses, geography, trade, and more.

http://quickfacts.census.gov—provides quick access to a wide variety of information about population characteristics at the state and county level.

- Utilize graphs and charts to emphasize specific market analysis. Discuss both present and future trends and describe how your company will capitalize on those trends.

DAY 19

Finish Your Business Plan

5. Strategies and Implementation

Detailed strategies that will be implemented to develop a successful and profitable business is vital. Explain your real estate goals and how you plan to achieve them.

6. Management Team

Whether you plan on establishing business as a sole proprietor, partnership, or corporation, it is important to include a resume of your management team. Include details of each member's qualifications, experience, duties they will perform.

List your professional and advisory support

Board of directors (if applicable)

Management advisory board (if applicable)

Attorney

Accountant

Insurance agent

Banker

Consultant

Mentor or business coach

7. Financial Projections

Considering real estate can be unstable at times, this can be one of the most challenging. Use the information from the previous sections to assess financial projections. If the presentation will be used to obtain financing, include sales forecasts for a minimum of three years.

**Once your business plan is complete, place the complete document in your bankbook under Tab 1. This should complete your bankbook to use for meetings with lenders and potential investing partners.

DAY 20

Start Networking

In order to know where to begin you must first understand what networking is and why it is important to grow your business. Networking in its purest form is simply talking to people, making connections and developing rapport to grow our circle of influence.

When you create valuable networking relationships, you a foundation of mutual trust, knowledge, experiences and resources to help one another grow your businesses by either referring one another or doing business directly with one another.

It works like this: If you do a good job, one customer might tell three to five of her colleagues, family and friends about you. Whereas, when you build a network of say 10 to 20 strong advocates, they may each tell only one person about your, however your "exposure" is now more than doubled - With the right network, the ultimate in "word of mouth" marketing takes place. You promote your network, and your network promotes you.

Begin researching organizations in your area to join in your area. This is the quickest way to add credible people to your team and increase your knowledge of real estate investing. I suggest you the websites of these two organizations and find a club to visit to decide which is best for you:

www.NationalREIA.com

www.REIA.org

Basic Networking Do's and Don'ts

Before you attend your first networking event (or if you have already started), consider these basic networking tips.

Tip 1—Don't Create the Wrong Business Cards

- Poor Quality with feather-like stock and bleeding ink

- "Mystery Business Card" if someone does not know immediately of service or product you offer

- No Logo or Logo that does not connect to business

- No unique selling proposition

- Oversized card

- Print that is too small to read

- Inadequate or poor use of color

- No physical address

- Lacking a website and/or email address

Tip 2—Create a Marketable Business Card

Your business card should have the following components:

- Logo that brands your company

- One line slogan to help people remember what you sell

- Web address and email address

- Readable font size

- Color, photo, or high gloss stock to stand out

- High quality card stock

- Current phone number and address

Tip 3—Creating your Unique Selling Proposition aka "Elevator Pitch"

Steps for development:

1. **List 3 Benefits your product or service** offers in terms of what your business does for your customer

2. **Be Unique**—your USP can be stated in your product itself, your offer, or your guarantee

3. **Be specific and offer proof**

4. **Solve an industry pain point** by indentifying needs that are unfulfilled in your industry or local market

5. **Condense into one clear, concise sentence** using words from any or all of steps 1-4

6. **USP should be 10-15 seconds**

Ex. Dominos Pizza: Fresh (benefit), hot (benefit) pizza (product) delivered to your door in 30 minutes or less (benefit)—or it's free!

Tip 4—Networking Don'ts

1. Don't be aggressive

2. Don't Monopolize

3. Don't remain with people you already know

4. Don't Use and Abuse with a "what's in it for me attitude"

Tip 5—Networking Do's

1. Make yourself stand out in a good way by looking professional

2. Be genuinely curious about the person you are meeting

3. Ask intelligent and caring questions

4. Pay attention to social graces—good personal hygiene, firm handshake, be courteous

5. Make proper eye contact

6. Make notes on business cards

7. Have specific goal (who you need to meet, how many new people you will meet)

8. Follow up

DAY 21

Get Social!

Social networking is defined as the grouping of individuals together into to specific groups, often like a small community or a neighborhood. Although social networking is possible in person, it is most popular online through websites. Social media is any form of online publication or presence that allows end users to engage in multi-directional conversations in or around the content on the website, such as LinkedIn, Twitter, Facebook, etc. I will focus on the most popular three to get started note there are numbers websites to launch your real estate investing business. Use each site as a medium to get to know more people and expand your business. On each you will set up a profile and be sure to include the following:

Professional picture

Short Bio that explains exactly what you do

Contact information such as email or cell phone

Your website, blogs, and videos

LinkedIn

LinkedIn is a business-oriented social networking site. Founded in December 2002 and launched in May 2003, it is mainly used for professional networking. LinkedIn had more than 60 million registered users, spanning more than 200 countries and territories worldwide.

www.Linkedin.com

Facebook

Founded in 2004, Facebook is a social networking website — a gathering spot, to connect with your friends and with your friends' friends. Facebook allows you to make new connections that share a common interest, expanding your personal network.

www.Facebook.com

Twitter

Twitter, created in 2006, is a social network aiming to enable its users to exchange news and opinions mostly concerning specific topics. The editor's "tweets" are sent via short message with a maximum length of 140 characters and can be subscribed to.

www.Twitter.com

CHAPTER 6

PROPERTY ANALYSIS

It's tangible, it's solid, it's beautiful.

It's artistic from my standpoint, and I just love real estate.

Donald Trump

Now it is time for the fun! You are now ready to start looking at properties that will build your portfolio.

I have one piece of advice to offer before you even step outside your door. It's about your "eyes"—your real estate eyes. You cannot afford, as an investor, to look at homes with the same eyes you'd bring to look at homes for you and your family to live in. *Do not* get emotionally attached when you look at properties. Your investment properties are like any other commodity—stocks, bonds, or for that matter, potatoes. Fall in love with the numbers. *Do not* fall in love with the property.

Learning to analyze properties is essential if you want to make money in real estate. Since you do, I have made it easier for you with forms you can use to record information on each home or multi-family unit that you consider. These forms also make it easier for you to look at the numbers to determine whether the properties you consider will offer viable cash flow. You will then make the decision, for each property in turn, whether to add it to your portfolio.

Over the next few days, you'll be looking at lots of properties. Lots. How many? It's up to you. But the number you should look at is: enough properties to enable you to make an offer on one, feeling sure, in your own well informed mind, that it's a smart and credible offer. You are on your way to acquiring your first investment property and becoming a real estate investor. Let's keep moving. You are almost there!

DAY 22

Evaluate Your Exit Strategies

There is a common phrase, *Begin With the End in Mind*. It means having a vision for finished product. In real estate investing, that essential step is an exit strategy. Your exit strategy is like deciding what dessert you are going to have before ordering your dinner. In essence it is your dessert because it is how you are going to profit from your deal.

Let's discuss the different exit strategies in detail and consider the pros and cons of each:

Wholesale

To *wholesale* is to place a property—normally a distressed one—under contract and then assign or resell the property to another investor. A wholesaler uses cash, lines of credit, or hard money loans. This allows for quick closings on properties that sometimes need extensive repair.

A wholesaler uses the principle that price overcomes all objections. If you can sell a property for a low enough price, the theory goes, it doesn't matter what's wrong with it—*somebody* will buy it. Wholesalers focus on developing two factors that play in their business:

- Finding deals

- Growing a network of investors to whom they can sell.

In the beginning, a wholesaler should not buy a property outright. The idea is: You put properties under contract with a contingency and focus on quickly selling the property for more money to other investors. If the property does not sell before you are expected to close, then your contingency allows you to walk away from the contract. A wholesaler is a middleman. The ideal situation to have is a good enough deal under contract that attracts other more established investors who will be glad to pay cash for it in a matter of days. Let's say you have a contract, at $55,000, on a 3-bedroom, 2-bathroom house that needs $10,000 in repairs and would likely sell—once repaired—for an estimated $100,000. You'd have some $35,000 in profit once you bought the house...repaired it...then sold it at $100,000—whenever you did. But suppose you had that house under contract at $55,000 and promptly sold it—within days—to another investor in your developed network—for $60,000. That, then, would be a quick profit of $5,000 to you. And *that* is what is called wholesaling.

The Flip

Property "flipping" refers to the purchase of real estate by an investor who quickly resells the property at a higher price in a short time—days to a few months. The technique is to look for properties, especially homes that are under-priced but offer values that can be marked up after some renovations. When a home sells at well under its fair market value, there are usually some specific cause or rationale at work—sometimes several of these in combination. Perhaps the home is being sold pursuant to a divorce, and the parties want the matter settled quickly. The owner may have lost his employment and needs the cash. Owners may be subsequently behind in mortgage payments, and are facing imminent foreclosure. Or perhaps the surviving family is selling the home, in the wake of the owner's death.

Lease Option

A lease option—also called a "rent-to-own purchase" or a "lease purchase"—is a lease combined with an option to purchase the property within a specified period, usually three years or less, at an agreed-upon price. The tenant pays an option fee, usually one percent to five percent of the purchase price, which is credited to the tenant when the purchase option is exercised. The tenant pays rent, plus an additional rent premium that is also credited to the purchase price. If the purchase option is not exercised, the tenant loses both the option fee that was the down payment and the rent premium.

Lease Purchase

The lease purchase offers an excellent exit strategy for two reasons. The tenant pays a large down payment and is responsible for most maintenance and repair costs. The downside is that there is a 75 to 80 per cent chance that the tenant will not exercise the option at the end of the term, so you will eventually have to find another tenant.

Seller Financing

In seller financing, the seller assumes the role of a bank and finances the buyer's purchase. The decision to provide seller financing, however, can be much more difficult. The virtue of seller financing is that it can make the difference between selling a house or not. On the other hand, seller financing means substantial risk in that the buyer could eventually default on the loan. Seller financing is a mode of selling no one should enter into lightly.

DAY 23

Implement Property Analysis Sheets

You will use the Property Analysis Sheets provided here to evaluate the properties you are considering for your investment portfolio. The three analysis sheets are:

- **Property Analysis Form**—to record information and observations on each property you are considering.

- **Property Rehab Analysis Form**—to analyze costs of minor and major improvements to prepare for retail or rental

- **Cash Flow Analysis Form**—to record the income and expenses on each property to calculate the monthly cash flow.

Become thoroughly familiar with all three forms so that you can fill them out with ease. Make plenty of copies of the forms before you start looking at the properties. You can also download these forms from www.jumpstartrealestateinvesting.com.

PROPERTY ANALYSIS FORM

1. OWNERSHIP AND PROPERTY LOCATION

Owner's Name_____ Telephone_____

Owner' Address_____

Property Address_____

2. PHYSICAL DESCRIPTION

Size in Square Feet _____ Bedrooms _____ Baths: Full___ Half___

Appliances   Refrigerator_____ Stove_____ Oven _____

Washer/Dryer_____ Water Softener _____

Microwave_____ Garbage Disposal _____

Dishwasher_____ Other_____

Basement_____ Attic_____ Porch_____ Utility Room_____

Garage_____ Den/Family Room_____ Lot Size_____ Zoning_____

Fireplace _____Window Coverings _____

Carpet _____ Construction _____ Age_____

Central AC _____ Heat _____ Largest Utility Bill _____

City Water/Septic _____ School District _____

Public Transportation _____ Taxes _____

Comments _____

3. OWNER'S SITUATION

How Long Owned? _____ How Long On Market? _____ Asking Price _____

Original Asking Price_____ Date of Price Change_____

Why Selling? _____ Needs Cash _____

How Much Cash? _____ Could Cash Be Spread Over Time? _____

What Owner Will Be Doing With Cash Received _____

Interest Rate _____

What Owner Likes Most About Property _____ Least _____

Comments _____

RENTAL ANALYSIS

Is Property Rented Now _____ To Whom? _____ Children? _____ Pets? _____

How Long? _____ Lease Or Month To Month? _____

Monthly Rent _____ Last Increase _____ Last Month's Rent _____

Security Deposit _____ Concessions _____

Potential Rental Income _____ Improvements Needed Before Renting
_____

Other Rents In Neighborhood _____ Rent Paid _____

Comments _____

5. FINANCING

First Mortgage   Lender _____ Balance _____

                         Interest Rate _____ Assumable _____ Payment _____

                         P.I.T.I.* _____ Constant _____

Second Mortgage   Lender _____ Balance _____

                         Interest Rate _____ Assumable _____ Payment _____

                         Constant _____

Other Liens _____

* Principal, Interest, Taxes, and Insurance

95

PROPERTY REHABILITATION ANALYSIS

Property Address _____

Owner's Name _____

Telephone Number (Home _____ (Work) _____

Age of Property _____

Listing Broker _____

Existing Loans and Status _____

Insured By _____ Amount _____

REHABILITATION NEEDED AND ESTIMATED COSTS

A. Rehabilitation Period Costs

Architect   _____

Legal Fees   _____

Accounting Fees   _____

Advertising   _____

Insurance   _____

Loan Fees   _____

Loan Interest   _____

Permits And Fees   _____

Real Estate Taxes   _____

Other   _____

Contingency   _____

Subtotal: Rehabilitation Period Costs   _____

B. Interior

Kitchen Appliances

       Stove   _____

       Refrigerator   _____

       Dishwasher   _____

       Washer/Dryer   _____

       Cabinets   _____

       Microwave   _____

       Other   _____

Total Appliances: _____

Master Bedroom   _____

Bedroom Two   _____

Bedroom Three   _____

Bedroom Four   _____

Bathroom One   _____

Bathroom Two   _____

Den   _____

Family Room   _____

Halls   _____

Floors   _____

Elevator   _____

Water Heater   _____

Water Softener   _____

Boiler   _____

Heating System   _____

Electrical   _____

Plumbing   _____

Fire Protection System   _____

Furniture/ Fixtures   _____

Other   _____

Contingency   _____

Subtotal: Interior   _____

C. Exterior

Roof   _____

Windows   _____

Doors   _____

Walls   _____

Trim   _____

Garage   _____

Chimney   _____

Yard   _____

Landscaping   _____

Well   _____

Septic Tank   _____

Sprinkler System   _____

Driveway   _____

Walkways   _____

Porch   _____

Steps _____

Pool/Pool Equipment _____

Light/Light Fixtures _____

Other _____

Contingency _____

Subtotal: Exterior _____

D. Amount Invested

First Mortgage _____

Second Mortgage _____

Third Mortgage _____

Other Liens _____

Back Payments _____

Back Taxes _____

Closing Costs _____

Estimated Costs to Sell _____

Other _____

Subtotal: Amount Invested _____

TOTAL COSTS EXCLUDING SELLER'S EQUITY (A+B+C+D) _____

_____

Estimated Selling Price Based On Comparisons _____

Less Amount Invested (Total Costs Excluding Sellers Equity) _____

Profit Before Cash Or Notes To Seller For Equity _____

Less Cash Or Notes To Seller _____

Estimated Gross Profit _____

CASH FLOW ANALYSIS

Gross Income:

Estimated Annual Gross Income _____

Other Income _____

Total Gross Income _____

Less Vacancy Allowance _____

Effective Gross Income _____

Expenses:

Taxes _____

Insurance _____

Water/Sewer _____

Garbage _____

Electricity _____

Licenses _____

Advertising _____

Supplies _____

Maintenance _____

Lawn _____

Snow Removal _____

Pest Control _____

Management Fee _____

Accounting/Legal _____

Miscellaneous _____

Gas _____

Pool _____

Budget For Replacements _____

Total Expenses _____

(A) Net Operating Income _____

Debt Service:

1st Mortgage _____

2nd Mortgage _____

3rd Mortgage _____

(B) Total Debt Service _____

Net Operating Income (A) – Total Debt Service (B) = Cash Flow

_____ - _____ = _____

Cash Flow _____

DAY 24

Analyze Properties

Visit five properties and complete analysis sheets on each property.

Property 1

Street Address

_____

City, State, Zip

_____

_____ Completed Analysis Sheets

_____ Overall rating for the property

(1-Poor, 2-Fair, 3-Average, 4-Good, 5-Excellent)

Property 2

Street Address

_____

City, State, Zip

_____

_____ Completed Analysis Sheets

_____ Overall rating for the property

(1-Poor, 2-Fair, 3-Average, 4-Good, 5-Excellent)

Property 3

Street Address

_____

City, State, Zip

_____

_____ Completed Analysis Sheets

_____ Overall rating for the property

(1-Poor, 2-Fair, 3-Average, 4-Good, 5-Excellent)

Property 4

Street Address

_____

City, State, Zip

_____

_____ Completed Analysis Sheets

_____ Overall rating for the property

(1-Poor, 2-Fair, 3-Average, 4-Good, 5-Excellent)

Property 5

Street Address

_____

City, State, Zip

_____

_____ Completed Analysis Sheets

_____ Overall rating for the property

(1-Poor, 2-Fair, 3-Average, 4-Good, 5-Excellent)

DAY 25

Analyze Properties

Visit five properties and complete analysis sheets on each property

Property 1

Street Address

_____

City, State, Zip

_____

_____ Completed Analysis Sheets

_____ Overall rating for the property

(1-Poor, 2-Fair, 3-Average, 4-Good, 5-Excellent)

Property 2

Street Address

_____

City, State, Zip

_____

_____ Completed Analysis Sheets

_____ Overall rating for the property

(1-Poor, 2-Fair, 3-Average, 4-Good, 5-Excellent)

Property 3

Street Address

_____

City, State, Zip

_____

_____ Completed Analysis Sheets

_____ Overall rating for the property

(1-Poor, 2-Fair, 3-Average, 4-Good, 5-Excellent)

Property 4

Street Address

_____

City, State, Zip

_____

_____ Completed Analysis Sheets

_____ Overall rating for the property

(1-Poor, 2-Fair, 3-Average, 4-Good, 5-Excellent)

Property 5

Street Address

_____

City, State, Zip

_____

_____ Completed Analysis Sheets

_____ Overall rating for the property

(1-Poor, 2-Fair, 3-Average, 4-Good, 5-Excellent)

DAY 26

Analyze Properties

Visit five properties and complete analysis sheets on each property

Property 1

Street Address

_____

City, State, Zip

_____

_____ Completed Analysis Sheets

_____ Overall rating for the property

(1-Poor, 2-Fair, 3-Average, 4-Good, 5-Excellent)

Property 2

Street Address

_____

City, State, Zip

_____

_____ Completed Analysis Sheets

_____ Overall rating for the property

(1-Poor, 2-Fair, 3-Average, 4-Good, 5-Excellent)

Property 3

Street Address

_____

City, State, Zip

_____

_____ Completed Analysis Sheets

_____ Overall rating for the property

(1-Poor, 2-Fair, 3-Average, 4-Good, 5-Excellent)

Property 4

Street Address

_____

City, State, Zip

_____

_____ Completed Analysis Sheets

_____ Overall rating for the property

(1-Poor, 2-Fair, 3-Average, 4-Good, 5-Excellent)

Property 5

Street Address

_____

City, State, Zip

_____

_____ Completed Analysis Sheets

_____ Overall rating for the property

(1-Poor, 2-Fair, 3-Average, 4-Good, 5-Excellent)

DAY 27

Make Offers

The past three days you have been looking at several potential properties and working the numbers on each one. Now you must decide which one you really want. In order for you to acquire your first investment property, you have to make an offer.

If you have been working with a real estate agent who has plenty of experience working with real estate investors or who is also a real estate investor in his own right, he will be able to guide you through this process with ease. Complete the process in these simple steps...

1. Choose the property on which you want to make an offer first.

2. Decide on a closing date.

3. Determine how much earnest money you are willing to commit (suggested: $250 to $1000).

4. Fill out an Offer to Purchase Real Estate contract.

5. Submit your contract to the appropriate owner or real estate agent.

6. Wait to see whether your offer is accepted.

CHAPTER 7

DETERMINE YOUR DESTINY

The victory of success is half won when one gains the habit of setting goals and achieving them. Even the most tedious chore will become endurable as you parade through each day convinced that every task, no matter how menial or boring, brings you closer to fulfilling your dreams

Og Mandino

Congratulations! For the past 27 days you have been working hard to get your real estate investment business off the ground. I hope you are proud of the positive steps you have made to create the future that you dream about. Even if you had some setbacks or became discouraged....its ok— as long as you keep moving forward. If life disrupts your plans, from this point on, don't quit. Success is closer than you think. How do I know? It's happened before....

An uncle of R U Darby was caught by the Gold Fever in the gold rush – days, and went west to Dig and Grow Rich. He had never heard that more gold had been mined from the brains of men than has ever been taken from the earth. He staked a claim and went to work with pick and shovel. The going was hard, but his lust for gold was definite.

*After weeks of labor, he was rewarded by the discovery of the shining ore. He needed machinery to bring the ore to the surface. Quietly, he covered up the mine, retraced his footsteps to his home in Williamsburg, Maryland, and told his relatives and a few neighbors of the **strike**. They got together money for the needed machinery, had it shipped. The uncle and Darby went back to work the mine.*

The first car of ore was mined, and shipped to smelter. The returns showed they had one of the richest mines in Colorado! A few more cars of that ore would clear the debts. Then would come the big killing in profits. Down went the drills. Up went the hopes of Darby and uncle. Then something happened. The vein of gold ore disappeared. They had come to the end of the rainbow, and the pot of gold was no longer there. They drilled on, desperately trying to pick up the vein again – all to no avail.

Finally they decided to QUIT.

They sold the machinery to a junk man for a few hundred dollars, and took the train back home. Some junk men are dumb, but not this one. He called in a mining engineer to look at the mine and do a little calculating. The engineer advised that the project had failed, because the owners were not familiar with fault lines. His calculations showed that the vein would be found Just Three Feet From Where The Darby's Had Stopped Drilling. That is exactly where it was found. The Junk man took millions of dollars in ore from the mine, because he knew enough to seek counsel before giving up.

This story is an excerpt from <u>Think and Grow Rich</u> by Napoleon Hill. It is a story of perseverance, which is essential to reach you long-term goals. One of the most common causes of failure is the habit of quitting when you are overtaken by *temporary defeat*. So I challenge you to be different. I guarantee you that you will encounter bumps in the road. Use these bumps to catapult you even closer to your dreams. Keep going, and whatever you do, don't quit!

DAY 28

Set Smart Goals

After you have a clear vision for your future, you can formulate your goals and action plans. Setting your goals properly is almost as important as the goals. A lot of people do not accomplish their goals because they do not set them properly. SMART goals contain all of the vital elements to maximize your success.

SMART stands for

Specific

Measurable

Attainable

Realistic

Timely

Specific

A specific goal has a much greater chance of being accomplished than a general goal. To set a specific goal you must answer the six "W" questions:

Who: Who is involved?

What: What do I want to accomplish?

Where: Identify a location.

When: Establish a time frame.

Which: Identify requirements and constraints.

Why: Specific reasons, purpose or benefits of accomplishing the goal.

Example: A general goal would be, "Get in shape." A specific goal would say, "Join a health club and workout 3 days a week"

Measurable

Establish concrete criteria for measuring progress toward the attainment of each goal you set. When you measure your progress, you stay on track, reach your target dates, and experience the exhilaration that spurs you on to continued effort required to reach your goal.

To determine if your goal is measurable; ask questions such as *How much? How many? How will I know when it is accomplished?*

Attainable

When you identify goals that are most important to you, you begin to figure out ways you can make them come true. You develop the attitudes, abilities, skills and financial capacity to reach them. You begin seeing previously overlooked opportunities to bring yourself closer to the achievement of your goals.

You may attain most any goal you set when you plan your steps wisely and establish a time frame that allows you to carry out those steps. Goals that may have seemed far away and out of reach eventually move closer and become attainable, not because your goals shrink but because you grow and expand to match them. When you list your goals you build your self-image. You see your-self as worthy of these goals, and develop the traits and personality that allow you to possess them.

Realistic

To be realistic, a goal must represent an objective toward which you are both willing and able to work. A goal can be both high and realistic; you are the only one who can decide just how high your goal should be. But be sure that every goal represents substantial progress. A high goal is frequently easier to reach than a low one because a low goal exerts low motivational force. Some of the hardest jobs you ever accomplished may actually seem easy simply because there were a labor of love.

Your goal is probably realistic if you truly believe that it can be accomplished. Additional ways to know if your goal is realistic is to determine if you have accomplished anything similar in the past or ask yourself what conditions would have to exist to accomplish this goal.

Timely

A goal should be grounded within a time frame. With no time frame tied to it there's no sense of urgency. If you want to buy 3 houses, when do you want to have them bought? Someday will not work, but if you anchor it within a timeframe, "by

May 6th," then you've set your unconscious mind into motion to begin working on the goal.

T can also stand for Tangible. A goal is tangible when you can experience it with one of the senses, which is taste, touch, smell, sight or hearing. When your goal is tangible, you have a better chance of making it specific and measurable and thus attainable.

Now that you know the correct way to set goals, it is time that you set some for the next 90 days—that is jumpstart real estate investing.

Real Estate Investing Goal 1

_____

_____

Date _____

Real Estate Investing Goal 2

_____

_____

Date _____

Business Goal 1

_____

_____

Date _____

Personal Goal 1

_____

_____

Date _____

Personal Goal 2

_____

_____

Date _____

Choose 5 Business Goals or Strategic Projects to focus on the Next 6 months

1. _____

2. _____

3. _____

4. _____

5. _____

Areas for Suggestion: Financial, Leadership, Systems, Sales, Marketing, Technology, Freedom, Balance, Income, Time Management.

DAY 29

Conquer Limiting Beliefs

What beliefs or fears are holding me or my real estate investing business back?

_____

_____

_____

_____

Have you ever tested these beliefs/fears for accuracy? Y/N _____

False assumptions lie at the root of most failures.

What positive thoughts will you tell yourself daily to conquer your fears?

_____

_____

_____

_____

What actions will you take daily to conquer your limiting beliefs?

_____

_____

_____

_____

DAY 30

Take My Advice

Did it seem like it took forever to get to Day 30? Congratulations you made it! I must warn you that it is just the beginning. You have proven to yourself that you can do this. Now it is time to take your game to next level. You are probably wondering what do I do from here? One of four things have happened...

1. You are still waiting on an answer from your offer

2. Your offer was not accepted

3. Your offer was accepted

4. You never submitted an offer

I hope it is one of the top three. If it is, you have done your homework and have everything planned out. Through experience you will find a model in real estate investing that you love. Once you do, keep doing it, perfect it, and find another form of real estate investing that you love so that you continue to grow as a professional while building wealth.

Now if you are number four, you have to figure out why. You may have to revisit Day 29 and conquer your fears. I would be lying to you if I told that I was not nervous my first few deals. I was even more excited about the possibilities that my newfound investment strategy would bring.

As your real estate coach, I urge you to get going! You have come this far so I know you can do it. Continue to surround yourself with positive people, believe in yourself, and take action!

Your future awaits......

ABOUT THE AUTHOR

Natasha Bowen is a profession- ally trained and certified busi- ness coach. She facilitates and leads clients through The Growth Coach's Strategic Mindset Process™. She earned her Bachelor of Science from Spelman College (Atlanta, GA) and her Masters in Business Administration from Union Uni- versity (Jackson, TN). Natasha is a licensed real estate affiliate broker and full-time real estate investor. With over 15 years of business experience as a sales execu- tive, real estate investor, and business owner, Nata- sha attributes her success to the principles she is now teaching and coaching to others.

www.JumpStartRealEstateInvesting.com

Coaching Packages

Educational Resources

Membership Forum

Free Downloads

www.ingramcontent.com/pod-product-compliance
Lightning Source LLC
Chambersburg PA
CBHW051541170526
45165CB00002B/832